My Stuff
Home Inventory Worksheets

JOE KIDD

INTRODUCTION

Experiencing a fire or storm loss is devastating, but imagine trying to list from memory every single item in your home that might be lost. That task is less daunting if you create a home inventory in advance and store it in a safe location. This is a three step process:

- Decide how and where you want to store the inventory.
- Take an inventory of the contents of your home.
- Third and possibly most important, keep the inventory up to date.

How and where you want to store the inventory.

Regardless of how you do it (written list, photos, videos,), keep your inventory along with receipts in a safe and secure location. The likely choices are:

- bank safe deposit box – the inconvenience of access may discourage frequent updates ,
- a relative's home – again access may discourage your updates
- personal computer – your computer could be damaged or destroyed
- smartphone – your phone could be loss or you might forget to transfer data to the new phone.

Better choices are:

- An inventory app for your smartphone or tablet
- a database or spreadsheets of inventory lists
- a simple word document with embedded photos or videos.

Each of these make it easy to keep up to date and have data stored remotely in online backup services, cloud storage accounts or even your personal email account. No matter how your where you store the inventory, make certain it is safe by using password protection or encryption.

CONTENTS

1 YOUR STUFF

Collecting your inventory

There are several ways to approach personal property inventory. The easiest of the approach taken will likely be the most incomplete. A complete inventory may take some time to create and could be updated over time. You will be surprised of the treasures you will find in your own home that you had not thought about. My personal choice starts with taking photographs of each room and then preparing a detailed property list.

Room by room photos.

The old saying "A picture is worth a thousand words" aptly describes my recommended method of starting an inventory. The process is as simple as a walk through your house. Start at your entry door and work your way through the house starting with main living spaces, followed by the kitchen, bedrooms, hallways and baths. Do not forget the garage and basement.

My approach is to stand in the room facing north, take a picture, then face east take a picture, followed by south and west. Then I face northeast, snap photo of the corner of the room and repeat until each corner is photographed. This will allow you of have a simple panoramic look at the whole. The same can be accomplished with a panoramic or video camera. The disadvantage of a video review is the speed and steadiness of the camera.

The following set of illustrations will demonstrate the process:

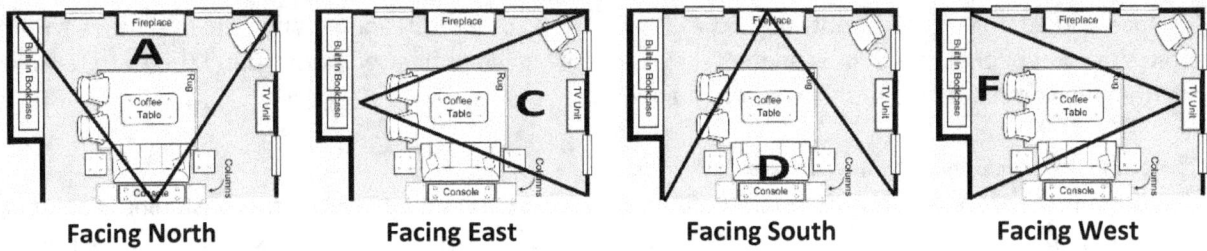

| Facing North | Facing East | Facing South | Facing West |

Try to capture as much of each wall as space allows. The corner photos will as capture part of the floor and ceiling because of the added depth of the room.

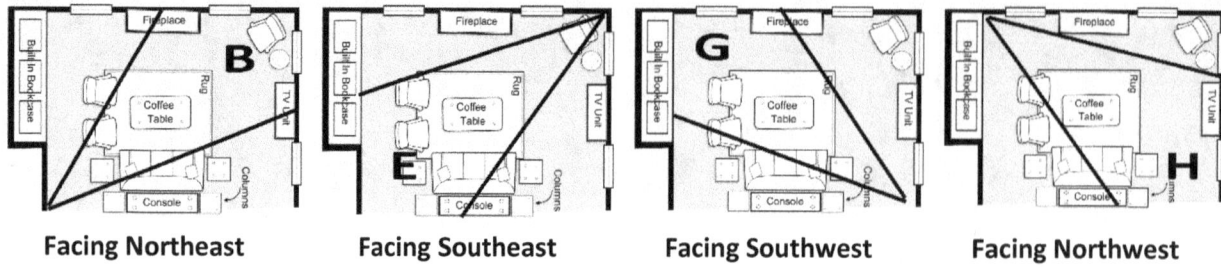

| Facing Northeast | Facing Southeast | Facing Southwest | Facing Northwest |

Once complete with room, repeat the process until all of the rooms have been photographed. Some rooms like baths and closet may not be large enough to need all eight photos. For instance my master room, I snap a photo at the door and another at the wall across from the door. This will have captured all of the contents of the room.

You may want to take a new set of photos for any room that you move around, redecorate and purchase new items for.

While on the subject of photos, this would be a good time to go outside and take pictures of the exterior using the same approach shown above. This capture all of the hidden features of the house. Additionally, I went to Google Maps and captured the satellite view of house and stored it the other photos.

Your inventory

To begin gathering your inventory, start in the room you took the first photographs. Using whatever system you decided upon, go item by item capturing the following details every visible item:

- description of the item,
- model number, if applicable
- serial number, if applicable
- year purchased
- amount paid and receipt if available.
- quantity, if more than one (i.e. end tables, lamps)
- comments

Don't forget the ceilings, floors and window coverings. This will be a time consuming, but all to important task. Don't become discouraged. To keep the task from being overwhelming, I processed one room each night until complete. At this point, don't inventory the contents of cabinets, closets and drawers.

Once you complete the inventory, you can keep it up to date by adding any new purchases to the room's list. Keep, photograph or scan the receipts of any newly purchased items. Don't forget to remove the item being replaced from the inventory if applicable.

Cabinets, closets cupboards and drawers

If the first part of the inventory felt daunting, the next part can be really time consuming. Cabinets, closet, cupboards and drawers can contain hundreds of items. To make this simpler, appendix A contents a variety of templates the can be used recording your inventory.

Once each of the templates are complete, safely secure the lists. A variety of storage avenues are available; electronic with cloud storage, paper stored in a safe deposit or even on your smart phone or tablet. My preference is electronic with both physical and cloud storage. Having a home business, my livelihood is contained on computers. I store all of my documents, these and everything else on a portable hard drive. The price for these storage devices as come down dramatically over the past few years. I perform daily backups to the hard drive and store it in a fire-rating safe. Additionally, I store my inventory documents inside of a draft email in my Gmail account. This allows for easy access to update or in the event it is needed. The email folder is even more secure than other cloud based options as long as you frequently change passwords and enable two-step authentication.

You are now probably thinking about how to keep the inventory worksheets up to date. I have a system where I keep all of my receipts for anything purchased for the house and on a monthly basis record all of the purchased items. Additionally, I scan the receipts for all big ticket items or take advantage of retailers that send receipts by email (Home Depot, Best Buy, Amazon, etc.) Samples of each worksheets in Appendix A.

Flight or Fight

One additional consideration, given the recent wildfires in the western U.S. and Canada, the massive destruction from tornados in the Midwest and flooding from hurricanes. You need to be prepared in the event of total destruction. The inventory process suggested before is inadequate in this regard.

Begin by getting access to the home appraisal from when you brought the house or last refinanced. Usually there is a sketch or diagram of the general layout of your house. Enlarge that to one room per sheet of paper. If the appraisal is not handy, you can sketch a diagram of each room. Go room by room, adding the overall dimensions and the location of all of the features of the room. This would include light switches, lighting, wall outlets and built in features. Taking pictures or making a video of the same is also a good approach.

One particular area to document is any built in or attached cabinetry. Bath and kitchen cabinetry come in a variety of depths, heights and lengths. Without proper documentation you may end with smaller cabinets. Make no mistake missing 2 inches of depth in a kitchen cabinet is big mistake. I learned from mine. Take pictures of your cabinets with a tape measure in the picture to prove the dimension. Quality of the cabinets and countertops can be proved by photos. I you don't plan for the worst, you will not get the best.

2 LIVING ROOM

Attach your photos here or just sketch the contents of the room

MY STUFF

Living Room	Qty	Description	Purchased	Cost

Living Room	Qty	Description	Purchased	Cost

MY STUFF

Living Room	Qty	Description	Purchased	Cost

3 FAMILY ROOM

Attach your photos here or just sketch the contents of the room

MY STUFF

Family Room	Qty	Description	Purchased	Cost

Family Room	Qty	Description	Purchased	Cost

MY STUFF

Family Room	Qty	Description	Purchased	Cost

4 KITCHEN

Attach your photos here or just sketch the contents of the room

MY STUFF

Kitchen	Qty	Description	Purchased	Cost

JOE KIDD

Kitchen	Qty	Description	Purchased	Cost

MY STUFF

Kitchen	Qty	Description	Purchased	Cost

5 MASTER BEDROOM

Attach your photos here or just sketch the contents of the room

MY STUFF

Master Bedroom	Qty	Description	Purchased	Cost

JOE KIDD

Master Bedroom	Qty	Description	Purchased	Cost

MY STUFF

Master Bedroom	Qty	Description	Purchased	Cost

6 BEDROOM 2

Attach your photos here or just sketch the contents of the room

MY STUFF

Bedroom 2	Qty	Description	Purchased	Cost

Bedroom 2	Qty	Description	Purchased	Cost

Bedroom 2	Qty	Description	Purchased	Cost

7 GUEST BEDROOM

Attach your photos here or just sketch the contents of the room

MY STUFF

Guest Bedroom	Qty	Description	Purchased	Cost

JOE KIDD

Guest Bedroom	Qty	Description	Purchased	Cost

MY STUFF

Guest Bedroom	Qty	Description	Purchased	Cost

8 MASTER BATH

Attach your photos here or just sketch the contents of the room

Master Bath	Qty	Description	Purchased	Cost

JOE KIDD

Master Bath	Qty	Description	Purchased	Cost

MY STUFF

Master Bath	Qty	Description	Purchased	Cost

9 BATHROOM

Attach your photos here or just sketch the contents of the room

MY STUFF

Bathroom	Qty	Description	Purchased	Cost

Bathroom	Qty	Description	Purchased	Cost

MY STUFF

Bathroom	Qty	Description	Purchased	Cost

10 OFFICE / HOBBY ROOM

Attach your photos here or just sketch the contents of the room

MY STUFF

Office / Hobby Room	Qty	Description	Purchased	Cost

JOE KIDD

Office / Hobby Room	Qty	Description	Purchased	Cost

MY STUFF

Office / Hobby Room	Qty	Description	Purchased	Cost

11 GARAGE / STORAGE

Attach your photos here or just sketch the contents of the room

MY STUFF

Garage / Storage	Qty	Description	Purchased	Cost

JOE KIDD

Garage / Storage	Qty	Description	Purchased	Cost

MY STUFF

Garage / Storage	Qty	Description	Purchased	Cost

12 LAUNDRY

Attach your photos here or just sketch the contents of the laundry room

Laundry	Qty	Description	Purchased	Cost

13 MISC 1

Attach your photos here or just sketch the contents of the room

Misc	Qty	Description	Purchased	Cost

MY STUFF

Misc	Qty	Description	Purchased	Cost

14 OTHER

47

JOE KIDD

Room	Item	Qty	Description	Purchased	Cost

MY STUFF

Room	Item	Qty	Description	Purchased	Cost

JOE KIDD

Room	Item	Qty	Description	Purchased	Cost

MY STUFF

Room	Item	Qty	Description	Purchased	Cost

JOE KIDD

Room	Item	Qty	Description	Purchased	Cost

MY STUFF

Room	Item	Qty	Description	Purchased	Cost

Room	Item	Qty	Description	Purchased	Cost

MY STUFF

Room	Item	Qty	Description	Purchased	Cost

JOE KIDD

Room	Item	Qty	Description	Purchased	Cost